D1457422

Geocaching Journal

and

Log Book

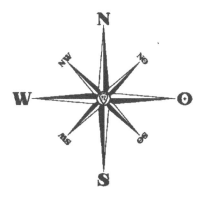

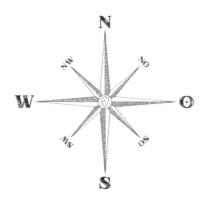

This Geocaching
Log Book Belongs
To This Awesome Person

_____

Date_____

Day of Week						
M	T	W	T	F	S	S

Time:_____

Location:_____

Latitude: _____

Longitude:_____

Difficulty:_____

Weather:_____

Quality of Cache

Party Members

Type of Container

Hints

Items Left or Removed

Notes

Date_____

	Day of Week					
M	T	W	T	F	S	S

Time:_____

Location:_____

Latitude: _____

Longitude:_____

Difficulty:_____

Weather:_____

Quality of Cache

Party Members

Type of Container

Hints

Items Left or Removed

Notes

Time:_____

Location:_____

Latitude: _____

Longitude:_____

Difficulty:_____

Weather:_____

Date_____

Day of Week						
M	T	W	T	F	S	S

Quality of Cache

Party Members

Type of Container

Hints

Items Left or Removed

Notes

Date_____

Day of Week						
M	T	W	T	F	S	S

Time:_____

Location:_____

Latitude: _____

Longitude:_____

Difficulty:_____

Weather:_____

Quality of Cache

....

....

....

....

....

....

Party Members

....

....

....

....

....

....

Type of Container

....

....

....

....

....

Hints

....

....

....

....

Items Left or Removed

....

....

....

....

Notes

Date_____

Day of Week						
M	T	W	T	F	S	S

Time:_____

Location:_____

Latitude: _____

Longitude:_____

Difficulty:_____

Weather:_____

Quality of Cache

....

....

....

....

....

....

....

Party Members

....

....

....

....

....

....

Type of Container

....

....

....

....

....

Hints

....

....

....

....

....

Items Left or Removed

....

....

....

....

....

Notes

Date_____

Day of Week						
M	T	W	T	F	S	S

Time:_____

Location:_____

Latitude: _____

Longitude:_____

Difficulty:_____

Weather:_____

Party Members

....

....

....

....

....

Hints

....

....

....

....

....

Quality of Cache

....

....

....

....

....

....

....

Type of Container

....

....

....

....

....

Items Left or Removed

....

....

....

....

....

Notes

Date_____

Day of Week						
M	T	W	T	F	S	S

Time:_____

Location:_____

Latitude: _____

Longitude:_____

Difficulty:_____

Weather:_____

Quality of Cache

Party Members

Type of Container

Hints

Items Left or Removed

Notes

Date_____

Day of Week						
M	T	W	T	F	S	S

Time:_____

Location:_____

Latitude: _____

Longitude:_____

Difficulty:_____

Weather:_____

Quality of Cache

Party Members

Type of Container

Hints

Items Left or Removed

Notes

Date_____

Day of Week						
M	T	W	T	F	S	S

Time:_____

Location:_____

Latitude: _____

Longitude:_____

Difficulty:_____

Weather:_____

Quality of Cache

Party Members

Type of Container

Hints

Items Left or Removed

Notes

Date_____

Day of Week						
M	T	W	T	F	S	S

Time:_____

Location:_____

Latitude: _____

Longitude:_____

Difficulty:_____

Weather:_____

Party Members

Quality of Cache

Type of Container

Hints

Items Left or Removed

Notes

Date_____

Day of Week						
M	T	W	T	F	S	S

Time:_____

Location:_____

Latitude:_____

Longitude:_____

Difficulty:_____

Weather:_____

Quality of Cache

Party Members

Type of Container

Hints

Items Left or Removed

Notes

Date_____

Day of Week						
M	T	W	T	F	S	S

Time:_____

Location:_____

Latitude: _____

Longitude:_____

Difficulty:_____

Weather:_____

Party Members

Hints

Quality of Cache

Type of Container

Items Left or Removed

Notes

Date_____

Day of Week						
M	T	W	T	F	S	S

Time:_____

Location:_____

Latitude: _____

Longitude:_____

Difficulty:_____

Weather:_____

Quality of Cache

Party Members

Type of Container

Hints

Items Left or Removed

Notes

Date_____

Day of Week						
M	T	W	T	F	S	S

Time:_____

Location:_____

Latitude: _____

Longitude:_____

Difficulty:_____

Weather:_____

Quality of Cache

Party Members

Type of Container

Hints

Items Left or Removed

Notes

Date_____

Day of Week						
M	T	W	T	F	S	S

Time:_____

Location:_____

Latitude: _____

Longitude:_____

Difficulty:_____

Weather:_____

Quality of Cache
....
....
....
....
....
....
....

Party Members
....
....
....
....
....

Type of Container
....
....
....
....
....

Hints
....
....
....
....

Items Left or Removed
....
....
....
....

Notes

Date_____

Day of Week						
M	T	W	T	F	S	S

Time:_____

Location:_____

Latitude: _____

Longitude:_____

Difficulty:_____

Weather:_____

Party Members

Hints

Quality of Cache

Type of Container

Items Left or Removed

Notes

Date_____

Day of Week						
M	T	W	T	F	S	S

Time:_____

Location:_____

Latitude: _____

Longitude:_____

Difficulty:_____

Weather:_____

Quality of Cache

Party Members

Type of Container

Hints

Items Left or Removed

Notes

Date_____

Day of Week						
M	T	W	T	F	S	S

Time:_____

Location:_____

Latitude: _____

Longitude:_____

Difficulty:_____

Weather:_____

Quality of Cache

....

....

....

....

....

....

Party Members

....

....

....

....

....

Type of Container

....

....

....

....

....

Hints

....

....

....

....

....

Items Left or Removed

....

....

....

....

....

Notes

Time:_____

Location:_____

Latitude: _____

Longitude:_____

Difficulty:_____

Weather:_____

Party Members

....

....

....

....

....

Date_____

Day of Week						
M	T	W	T	F	S	S

Quality of Cache

....

....

....

....

....

....

....

Type of Container

....

....

....

....

....

Hints

....

....

....

....

Items Left or Removed

....

....

....

....

Notes

Date_____

Day of Week						
M	T	W	T	F	S	S

Time:_____

Location:_____

Latitude: _____

Longitude:_____

Difficulty:_____

Weather:_____

Quality of Cache
....
....
....
....
....
....

Party Members
....
....
....
....
....
....

Type of Container
....
....
....
....
....

Hints
....
....
....
....
....

Items Left or Removed
....
....
....
....

Notes

Date_____

Day of Week						
M	T	W	T	F	S	S

Time:_____

Location:_____

Latitude: _____

Longitude:_____

Difficulty:_____

Weather:_____

Quality of Cache

Party Members

Type of Container

Hints

Items Left or Removed

Notes

Date_____

Day of Week						
M	T	W	T	F	S	S

Time:_____

Location:_____

Latitude: _____

Longitude:_____

Difficulty:_____

Weather:_____

Quality of Cache

Party Members

Type of Container

Hints

Items Left or Removed

Notes

Date_____

Day of Week						
M	T	W	T	F	S	S

Time:_____

Location:_____

Latitude: _____

Longitude:_____

Difficulty:_____

Weather:_____

Quality of Cache

....

....

....

....

....

....

Party Members

....

....

....

....

....

....

Type of Container

....

....

....

....

....

Hints

....

....

....

....

....

Items Left or Removed

....

....

....

....

Notes

Date_____

Day of Week						
M	T	W	T	F	S	S

Time:_____

Location:_____

Latitude: _____

Longitude:_____

Difficulty:_____

Weather:_____

Quality of Cache

....

....

....

....

....

....

Party Members

....

....

....

....

....

....

Type of Container

....

....

....

....

....

Hints

....

....

....

....

....

Items Left or Removed

....

....

....

....

....

Notes

Date_____

Day of Week						
M	T	W	T	F	S	S

Time:_____

Location:_____

Latitude: _____

Longitude:_____

Difficulty:_____

Weather:_____

Quality of Cache

Party Members

Type of Container

Hints

Items Left or Removed

Notes

Date_____

Day of Week						
M	T	W	T	F	S	S

Time:_____

Location:_____

Latitude: _____

Longitude:_____

Difficulty:_____

Weather:_____

Quality of Cache
....
....
....
....
....
....
....

Party Members
....
....
....
....
....
....

Type of Container
....
....
....
....
....

Hints
....
....
....
....
....

Items Left or Removed
....
....
....
....

Notes

Time:_____

Location:_____

Latitude: _____

Longitude:_____

Difficulty:_____

Weather:_____

Date_____

Day of Week						
M	T	W	T	F	S	S

Quality of Cache

....

....

....

....

....

....

Party Members

....

....

....

....

....

Type of Container

....

....

....

....

....

Hints

....

....

....

....

Items Left or Removed

....

....

....

....

Notes

Date_____

Day of Week						
M	T	W	T	F	S	S

Time:_____

Location:_____

Latitude: _____

Longitude:_____

Difficulty:_____

Weather:_____

Quality of Cache

Party Members

Type of Container

Hints

Items Left or Removed

Notes

Date_____

Day of Week						
M	T	W	T	F	S	S

Time:_____

Location:_____

Latitude: _____

Longitude:_____

Difficulty:_____

Weather:_____

Quality of Cache

....

....

....

....

....

....

Party Members

....

....

....

....

....

....

Type of Container

....

....

....

....

....

Hints

....

....

....

....

....

Items Left or Removed

....

....

....

....

Notes

Date_____

Day of Week						
M	T	W	T	F	S	S

Time:_____

Location:_____

Latitude: _____

Longitude:_____

Difficulty:_____

Weather:_____

Party Members

....

....

....

....

....

Hints

....

....

....

....

....

Quality of Cache

....

....

....

....

....

....

Type of Container

....

....

....

....

Items Left or Removed

....

....

....

....

Notes

Date_____

Day of Week						
M	T	W	T	F	S	S

Time:_____

Location:_____

Latitude: _____

Longitude:_____

Difficulty:_____

Weather:_____

Quality of Cache

....

....

....

....

....

....

Party Members

....

....

....

....

....

Type of Container

....

....

....

....

Hints

....

....

....

....

Items Left or Removed

....

....

....

....

Notes

Date_____

Day of Week						
M	T	W	T	F	S	S

Time:_____

Location:_____

Latitude: _____

Longitude:_____

Difficulty:_____

Weather:_____

Quality of Cache

Party Members

Type of Container

Hints

Items Left or Removed

Notes

Date_____

Day of Week						
M	T	W	T	F	S	S

Time:_____

Location:_____

Latitude: _____

Longitude:_____

Difficulty:_____

Weather:_____

Quality of Cache

....

....

....

....

....

....

Party Members

....

....

....

....

....

Type of Container

....

....

....

....

....

Hints

....

....

....

....

....

Items Left or Removed

....

....

....

....

....

Notes

Date_____

Day of Week						
M	T	W	T	F	S	S

Time:_____

Location:_____

Latitude: _____

Longitude:_____

Difficulty:_____

Weather:_____

Quality of Cache

Party Members

Type of Container

Hints

Items Left or Removed

Notes

Date_____

Day of Week						
M	T	W	T	F	S	S

Time:_____

Location:_____

Latitude: _____

Longitude:_____

Difficulty:_____

Weather:_____

Quality of Cache

....

....

....

....

....

....

Party Members

....

....

....

....

....

....

Type of Container

....

....

....

....

....

Hints

....

....

....

....

....

Items Left or Removed

....

....

....

....

Notes

Date_____

Day of Week						
M	T	W	T	F	S	S

Time:_____

Location:_____

Latitude: _____

Longitude:_____

Difficulty:_____

Weather:_____

Party Members

Quality of Cache

Type of Container

Hints

Items Left or Removed

Notes

Date_____

Day of Week						
M	T	W	T	F	S	S

Time:_____

Location:_____

Latitude: _____

Longitude:_____

Difficulty:_____

Weather:_____

Quality of Cache

....

....

....

....

....

....

Party Members

....

....

....

....

....

....

Type of Container

....

....

....

....

....

Hints

....

....

....

....

Items Left or Removed

....

....

....

....

Notes

Date_____

Day of Week						
M	T	W	T	F	S	S

Time:_____

Location:_____

Latitude: _____

Longitude:_____

Difficulty:_____

Weather:_____

Quality of Cache

....
....
....
....
....
....

Party Members

....
....
....
....
....
....

Type of Container

....
....
....
....
....

Hints

....
....
....
....
....

Items Left or Removed

....
....
....
....

Notes

Date_____

Day of Week						
M	T	W	T	F	S	S

Time:_____

Location:_____

Latitude: _____

Longitude:_____

Difficulty:_____

Weather:_____

Quality of Cache

Party Members

Type of Container

Hints

Items Left or Removed

Notes

Date_____

Day of Week						
M	T	W	T	F	S	S

Time:_____

Location:_____

Latitude: _____

Longitude:_____

Difficulty:_____

Weather:_____

Quality of Cache

Party Members

Type of Container

Hints

Items Left or Removed

Notes

Date_____

Day of Week						
M	T	W	T	F	S	S

Time:_____

Location:_____

Latitude: _____

Longitude:_____

Difficulty:_____

Weather:_____

Quality of Cache

Party Members

Type of Container

Hints

Items Left or Removed

Notes

Date_____

Day of Week						
M	T	W	T	F	S	S

Time:_____

Location:_____

Latitude: _____

Longitude:_____

Difficulty:_____

Weather:_____

Party Members
....
....
....
....
....
....

Hints
....
....
....
....

Quality of Cache
....
....
....
....
....
....

Type of Container
....
....
....
....
....

Items Left or Removed
....
....
....
....

Notes

Date_____

Day of Week						
M	T	W	T	F	S	S

Time:_____

Location:_____

Latitude: _____

Longitude:_____

Difficulty:_____

Weather:_____

Quality of Cache

Party Members

Type of Container

Hints

Items Left or Removed

Notes

Date_____

Day of Week						
M	T	W	T	F	S	S

Time:_____

Location:_____

Latitude: _____

Longitude:_____

Difficulty:_____

Weather:_____

Quality of Cache

Party Members

Type of Container

Hints

Items Left or Removed

Notes

Date_____

Day of Week						
M	T	W	T	F	S	S

Time:_____

Location:_____

Latitude: _____

Longitude:_____

Difficulty:_____

Weather:_____

Quality of Cache

....
....
....
....
....
....
....

Party Members

....
....
....
....
....
....

Type of Container

....
....
....
....
....

Hints

....
....
....
....
....

Items Left or Removed

....
....
....
....

Notes

Date_____

Day of Week						
M	T	W	T	F	S	S

Time:_____

Location:_____

Latitude: _____

Longitude:_____

Difficulty:_____

Weather:_____

Quality of Cache

Party Members

Type of Container

Hints

Items Left or Removed

Notes

Date_____

Day of Week						
M	T	W	T	F	S	S

Time:_____

Location:_____

Latitude: _____

Longitude:_____

Difficulty:_____

Weather:_____

Quality of Cache

....

Party Members

Type of Container

Hints

Items Left or Removed

Notes

Date_____

Day of Week						
M	T	W	T	F	S	S

Time:_____

Location:_____

Latitude: _____

Longitude:_____

Difficulty:_____

Weather:_____

Party Members

....
....
....
....
....

Hints

....
....
....
....

Quality of Cache

....
....
....
....
....
....
....

Type of Container

....
....
....
....

Items Left or Removed

....
....
....
....

Notes

Time:_____

Location:_____

Latitude: _____

Longitude:_____

Difficulty:_____

Weather:_____

Date_____

Day of Week						
M	T	W	T	F	S	S

Quality of Cache

Party Members

Type of Container

Hints

Items Left or Removed

Notes

Date_____

Day of Week						
M	T	W	T	F	S	S

Time:_____

Location:_____

Latitude: _____

Longitude:_____

Difficulty:_____

Weather:_____

Quality of Cache
....
....
....
....
....
....

Party Members
....
....
....
....
....
....

Type of Container
....
....
....
....
....

Hints
....
....
....
....
....

Items Left or Removed
....
....
....
....
....

Notes

Date_____

Day of Week						
M	T	W	T	F	S	S

Time:_____

Location:_____

Latitude: _____

Longitude:_____

Difficulty:_____

Weather:_____

Quality of Cache
....
....
....
....
....
....

Party Members
....
....
....
....
....
....

Type of Container
....
....
....
....
....

Hints
....
....
....
....
....

Items Left or Removed
....
....
....
....
....

Notes

Date_____

Day of Week						
M	T	W	T	F	S	S

Time:_____

Location:_____

Latitude:_____

Longitude:_____

Difficulty:_____

Weather:_____

Quality of Cache

Party Members

Type of Container

Hints

Items Left or Removed

Notes

Date_____

Day of Week						
M	T	W	T	F	S	S

Time:_____

Location:_____

Latitude: _____

Longitude:_____

Difficulty:_____

Weather:_____

Quality of Cache

Party Members

Type of Container

Hints

Items Left or Removed

Notes

Date_____

Day of Week						
M	T	W	T	F	S	S

Time:_____

Location:_____

Latitude: _____

Longitude:_____

Difficulty:_____

Weather:_____

Quality of Cache

....

....

....

....

....

....

Party Members

....

....

....

....

....

....

Type of Container

....

....

....

....

Hints

....

....

....

....

....

Items Left or Removed

....

....

....

....

Notes

Date_____

Day of Week						
M	T	W	T	F	S	S

Time:_____

Location:_____

Latitude: _____

Longitude:_____

Difficulty:_____

Weather:_____

Quality of Cache

....

....

....

....

....

....

Party Members

....

....

....

....

....

....

Type of Container

....

....

....

....

....

Hints

....

....

....

....

Items Left or Removed

....

....

....

....

Notes

Date _____

Day of Week						
M	T	W	T	F	S	S

Time: _____

Location: _____

Latitude: _____

Longitude: _____

Difficulty: _____

Weather: _____

Quality of Cache

....

....

....

....

....

....

Party Members

....

....

....

....

....

....

Type of Container

....

....

....

....

....

....

Hints

....

....

....

....

Items Left or Removed

....

....

....

....

Notes

Date_____

Day of Week						
M	T	W	T	F	S	S

Time:_____

Location:_____

Latitude: _____

Longitude:_____

Difficulty:_____

Weather:_____

Quality of Cache

....
....
....
....
....
....

Party Members

....
....
....
....
....

Type of Container

....
....
....
....
....

Hints

....
....
....
....

Items Left or Removed

....
....
....
....

Notes

Date_____

Day of Week						
M	T	W	T	F	S	S

Time:_____

Location:_____

Latitude: _____

Longitude:_____

Difficulty:_____

Weather:_____

Quality of Cache
....
....
....
....
....
....
....

Party Members
....
....
....
....
....

Type of Container
....
....
....
....
....

Hints
....
....
....
....
....

Items Left or Removed
....
....
....
....

Notes

Date_____

Day of Week						
M	T	W	T	F	S	S

Time:_____

Location:_____

Latitude: _____

Longitude:_____

Difficulty:_____

Weather:_____

Quality of Cache

Party Members

Type of Container

Hints

Items Left or Removed

Notes

Date_____

Day of Week						
M	T	W	T	F	S	S

Time:_____

Location:_____

Latitude: _____

Longitude:_____

Difficulty:_____

Weather:_____

Quality of Cache
....
....
....
....
....
....

Party Members
....
....
....
....
....
....

Type of Container
....
....
....
....
....

Hints
....
....
....
....
....

Items Left or Removed
....
....
....
....
....

Notes

Date_____

Day of Week						
M	T	W	T	F	S	S

Time:_____

Location:_____

Latitude: _____

Longitude:_____

Difficulty:_____

Weather:_____

Party Members
....
....
....
....
....
....

Hints
....
....
....
....

Quality of Cache
....
....
....
....
....
....
....

Type of Container
....
....
....
....
....

Items Left or Removed
....
....
....
....

Notes

Date_____

Day of Week						
M	T	W	T	F	S	S

Time:_____

Location:_____

Latitude: _____

Longitude:_____

Difficulty:_____

Weather:_____

Party Members

_____

_____

_____

_____

_____

Hints

_____

_____

_____

_____

Quality of Cache

_____

_____

_____

_____

_____

_____

Type of Container

_____

_____

_____

_____

_____

Items Left or Removed

_____

_____

_____

_____

Notes